MY HANDS

By

Noah Messiah

<u>JOURNAL JOY</u>

An Imprint of Journal Joy Publishers

www.thejournaljoy.com

Copyright © 2022 by Noah Messiah

An Imprint of Journal Joy Publishers

All rights reserved. Printed in the United States of America. No part of this book may be reproduced, distributed, or transmitted in any form or by any means, without the authors' prior written permission, except in the case of brief quotations embodied in critical reviews and specific other noncommercial uses permitted by copyright law.

For information on publishing, contact Journal Joy at Info@thejournaljoy.com.

www.thejournaljoy.com

Summary:

Hardcover ISBN: 978-1-957751-04-7

Ebook ISBN: 978-1-957751-03-0

Edited by: Riel Felice

Author Email: Noahmessiah2014@gmail.com

First paperback edition, 2022

DEDICATION:

To my best friend, CJ:

May your hands forever be your voice when you can't find the words,
and may your actions speak to the strength of your heart.

I love going on new adventures with my family!

There is a lot happening here today!

A lot of people are holding up signs.

I don't understand it all, but they are telling me who I am.

They seem to be arguing about what path to take.

Sometimes, I get mad because I just don't understand.

When I am feeling bad,
my brother comforts me.

I show who I am with my hands.

I can do a lot of amazing things with my hands!

I feel excited to see all that I am able to be.

When I play with others, I am a good friend.

When I build, I am an engineer.

When I race, I am an athlete.

When I draw, I am an artist.

When I cook, I am a chef.

ABOUT THE AUTHOR

Noah Cole was born in Amberg, Germany to an active duty military family in 2014. It wasn't until he, his mom, and his brother moved to America that he began, at a very young age, to understand that society often tried to stereotype him and his family. Labels were quickly placed on him to identify who he was as a Hispanic and Black child in America, as well as on his brother, who has special needs. As a result of his mother's teaching, he was empowered to find his voice and did not want to be confined to a box of who others felt he was supposed to be. He wanted to spread the message that one's color, gender, ability, or circumstance does not define who they are. Rather, who a person chooses to be through their actions and character demonstrates who they truly are.

www.ingramcontent.com/pod-product-compliance
Lightning Source LLC
Chambersburg PA
CBHW041406010526
44107CB00015B/1096